PATCHWORK
FOLK ART

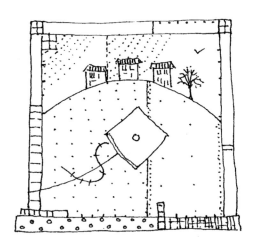

PATCHWORK FOLK ART

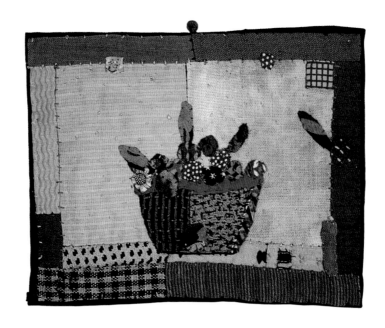

Using Appliqué & Quilting Techniques

JANET BOLTON

Photography by Sandra Lousada

MUSEUM QUILTS

Published by Museum Quilts (UK) Inc.
254-258 Goswell Road, London EC1V 7EB

Editor: Ljiljana Ortolja-Baird
Designer: Bet Ayer

A CIP catalogue record for this book is available from the British Library

ISBN: 1-897954-54-9

Printed in Singapore by Star Standard Industries Pte. Ltd.

For Paul, Fran and Ali

Contents

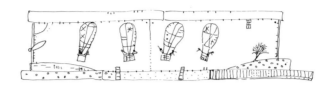

20.5 x 16cm / 8 x 6 ¹/₄in

Two Giraffes

Introduction

This book describes a personal way of making pictures. Throughout childhood I enjoyed making things, drawing and painting, collecting and arranging objects. As children, each autumn we collected seeds and berries to make specimen boxes, each item being arranged and labelled in box lids. It became a favourite activity, and I spent many hours ordering my collection until I was happy with its appearance. The memory of this childhood enjoyment is one of the reasons I believe that today I prefer to work with fabric rather than paint. Manipulating fabric allows me the same freedom of lifting, replacing and reorganizing.

Growing up in Lancashire, England the appreciation of fabric was part of everyday life. People felt cloth, tugged it about a bit, and commented on its different qualities. I remember spending happy times as a child playing with swatches of fabric samples when my father visited the tailors. Fabric holds its own evocative memories, it resonates with vitality. Who made it? How was it made? Where did it come from? How was it used – a summer dress, a suit for best, a wedding gown or a table cloth? Who gave it to me?

But more than this, using fabric links my work to the great folk art and needlework traditions of patchwork and appliqué. Fabric pictures in the past were frequently made with whatever was at hand and sometimes the most beautiful works of art were created, lifting the spirit of both maker and user with their presence in everyday life. With limited materials, and often in the most difficult conditions, a creative spirit would stitch and colour the most threadbare of fabrics and make for themselves and their family something both beautiful and functional. I am sure that in the past, making a quilt was a much needed excuse for picture making.

Making pictures is an age-old human preoccupation, and today many of us are in the fortunate position of not needing any excuse for indulging in this satisfying activity, yet most people abandon it after childhood. I suspect we are left stranded at a stage of 'seeing' a good picture as one that has true photographic likeness, and therefore are unable to relax and enjoy the process because we cannot make our pictures fit this limiting formula.

My work requires no special sewing skills. The techniques I use are very simple and the materials needed are readily available. In fact, a small collection of fabrics, the contents of a sewing basket, and an uncluttered kitchen table are all you need to get started. Everybody can wield a needle. The skill is not in how you sew but rather in what you sew. Clumsy stitches will spoil a picture but beautiful stitching alone cannot make an interesting picture. The secret is to take time, to watch how the shapes and composition evolve, and to be able to make adjustments as you go along.

There are two paths that can be followed in picture making. One involves trying to realize a fixed idea. The second relies on spontaneous development, on suddenly seeing, for instance, a new relationship between shape and colour and capturing that gift to change your course of direction. I like to think that my work informs me, that I am attentive to its growth, that I nurture it. I am forever surprised and delighted by its unexpected turns, and happily develop them.

My hope is that describing the working methods I enjoy will tempt others to try for themselves, and encourage artists-in-the-making to 'pick up the threads' and return to picture making with a fresh eye, so adding to the long, rich, and diverse tradition with their own work.

8¹/₂ x 7¹/₂in

Rag Doll and the Doll's House

CHAPTER ONE

Inspirations

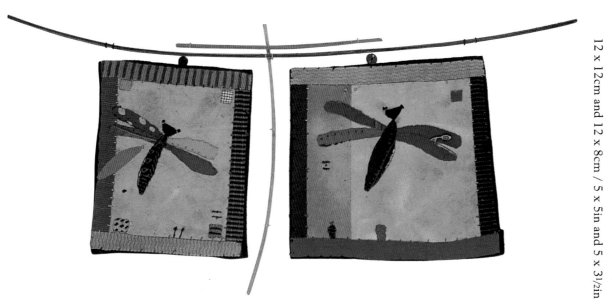

12 x 12cm and 12 x 8cm / 5 x 5in and 5 x 3¹⁄₂in

Two Dragonflies

Inspirations and ideas can come from many sources. They can spring to mind unexpectedly, or be deliberately sought. A new idea can suggest itself when you are busy doing other things, and does not always come from visual experiences. Atmospheres, feelings, half-forgotten memories can all play their part. A familiar object seen from an unusual position can set your mind racing. A combination of immediate events and past experiences can join to suggest a new idea, and send you rushing to make a note or get to work.

A chance positioning of basket cane, two horizontal across one vertical piece, reminded me of a dragonfly, and this set me to work on an old theme I hadn't used for years. Sometimes the ideas you have in mind work when you come to try them out, sometimes they don't, but it is always very enjoyable to see what happens – and often very surprising.

My greatest inspiration came when I happened on an exhibition of work by Elizabeth Allen. At art school in the early '60s I had been introduced to a way of working with textiles that focused on manipulating the physical properties of fabric, creating heavy and textured wall hangings. In contrast, Elizabeth Allen was using fabric with a purely pictorial intent. Her pictures are careful arrangements of flat, interlocking shapes.

Population Explosion by Elizabeth Allen
British Folk Art Collection, Bath. © Peter Moores Foundation 1994

42 x 29cm / 16 1/2 x 11 1/2in

She worked with materials that she had at hand, using skills developed over a lifetime of earning a living as a seamstress. The images, some of them disturbing, transcend the quiet, unassuming cloth from which they were made. I was not inspired to make similar images, but seeing fabric, the material that I loved to handle, used with such force and directness encouraged me to reassess how I was working.

My interest in textiles as a working medium was reinforced by the 'discovery' of quilts and Navaho eye-dazzler rugs. The outstanding colour and design of these unsung masterpieces were now being appreciated for their similarity to contemporary abstract painters. Quilts and rugs which had long been a love of mine were now being displayed in the same way as a painting, and appreciated for their aesthetic value, apart from their function.

1 4

Navaho eye-dazzler rug

Choosing to work with fabric, patchwork and appliqué are an obvious and wonderful source of inspiration, but they are only one of many that I draw from. Images made with wood, clay, paint, pastel and pencil often have qualities that are particularly appealing, qualities that I would like to capture in my work.

Local museums are a great source of ideas, containing a variety of objects made from a wide range of materials. Prehistoric tools, geological specimens, domestic artefacts, paintings, furniture, products from industry can offer a feast of colour, shape and design that may well spark off ideas for an interpretation of your own. A primitive hooked rug that I saw at the American Folk Art Museum in Bath inspired *Lion Amongst the Flowers*.

17 x 10cm / 7 x 4in

Lion Amongst the Flowers

Even if you don't have easy access to museums and galleries, many shops sell affordable items from all over the world that can be taken home as a constant inspiration. Making pictures of favourite objects can be very satisfying, and often very successful, for knowing them well will help you capture what it is about them that you like.

A personal collection of small toys has provided me with endless inspiration. Toys both old and new, some made by craftspeople working today, have been incorporated into my pictures.

In *Garden for a Sacred Cow*, I placed the small painted wooden cow on top of the frame as part of the composition.

23 x 23cm / 9 x 9in

Garden for a Sacred Cow

17

Children's work can hold great appeal. *The Snowman* was inspired by a wax crayon drawing made by my daughter when she was five. The element I chose to incorporate in my picture was the coloured line around the snowman. Often it is only part of a picture or object that provides the inspiration and frequently then it is used in a different way than in the original.

The simple shapes of *Two Angels Gliding By* in Chapter 5 also came to mind when looking at children's work. I had been drawing carved angels in my local museum and somehow couldn't get beyond the intricate surface patterns on the carving. My drawings did not translate comfortably into fabric. It is so easy to be dazzled by possibilities unsuitable for your own work. Working with school children one Christmas, I found the key to making 'my' angels. The children were using simple block shapes that were much more appropriate for my work. The absorbing study and drawing at the museum was time well spent, for it takes time to isolate those qualities that will best help your work. The process of stripping back to the essentials is a wonderful experience and helps you appreciate other works, as well as recognize exactly what it is about your own way of working that you enjoy.

Many people can visit an area, be inspired by the landscape around them and start work on a picture straight away. This has never worked for me. I have to wait for ideas to percolate. I may notice a new element and incorporate it immediately into an existing theme, but the theme itself will have taken time to develop. Places and activities I have seen over many years become recurring images.

25 x 19cm / 9 3/4 x 7 1/2in

Snowman drawing

16 x 16cm / 6¹/₄ x 6¹/₄in

The Snowman

Time and time again, I return to kite flying, probably because I live close by a great kite-flying area, and see them regularly. I can remember deciding on the composition of this picture whilst watching a kite being flown, profiled against land. I realized that all my previous pictures had depicted the kites against the sky.

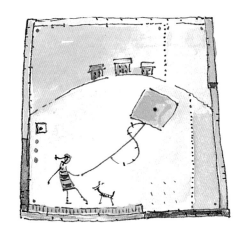

An important point to emphasize here is that you don't need to recreate exactly what you see. The scenes I observe are a starting point, an idea to set me thinking. I then go home and compose my picture in a way that pleases me, using some elements and discarding others. Even when you are deliberately trying to depict an actual scene, don't be frightened to rearrange the elements. You are making a new and different reality, and can do just what you like.

Careful observation can feed your imagination constantly, and drawing can provide you with a great visual reminder. If you are unsure about your ability to draw, think of your sketch as a series of notes.

For example, in drawing a sheep, observe the size of the head, how and where the horn fits, the position of the eye and what shape it is. Each observation, instead of being recorded with words, is noted graphically. You may not use the information precisely. For instance, in your picture of a sheep you may want to emphasize the bulk of the body and so choose to make the head significantly smaller. Collecting visual notes will help you to become more observant, and it is usually easier to make expressive departures from a subject that has been well observed.

When visiting the Yorkshire Dales, I am always struck by the wonderful colour harmonies of sky, land, buildings, animals, trees all so closely blended together. My sister-in-law, who lives in the Dales, dyed some fabrics for me from local plants. Inspired by her gift and my associations with the area, I conceived *Barn on the Moors* with its delicate tonal contrasts.

42 x 38cm / 16½ x 15in

Barn on the Moors

A commission can prove very stimulating in encouraging new directions in my work. To help celebrate the 25th anniversary of the Oxford Gallery I was asked to submit a series of pictures that reflected the historic university city. This exercise compelled me to think about a completely different set of ideas and resulted in an exciting new body of work as well as furthering existing themes. Seeing a photograph of college Masters in their scarlet gowns inspired me to make *One Don*.

RIGHT: *One Don*

20.5 x 15cm / 8 x 6in

20.5 x 15cm / 8 x 6in

Whilst working on this piece I was reminded of the famous painting by Scottish artist Sir Henry Raeburn, *Reverend Robert Walker Skating on Duddinston Lock*. From this prompt a second picture emerged. I humorously titled my picture *Don Skating on Isis Lock* to echo the formality of the original title and to acknowledge the visual link between the two pictures.

LEFT: *Don Skating on Isis Lock*

The owl is a favourite motif of mine and over the years I have made many pictures in honour of this wise old bird. Placed within the context of Oxford, an ancient seat of learning, the owl as a symbol of wisdom flying over the city skyline seemed particularly appropriate. The device of using specific architectural references was new to my work and very exciting.

16.5 x 10cm / 6½ x 4in

One Winter Night

I am sometimes asked if I worry about running out of ideas. The very opposite is true, for one idea leads to another, and the more time you spend making pictures, the more likely are you to be anxious to get on with the next. That is why I enjoy working around themes, for there is no way that I could explore all my ideas in just one picture. Some ideas work well and translate rapidly into a picture, some don't, and some lie forgotten for years. It's much more difficult to start a new theme, but once started any problems of what to explore next will soon disappear.

Workshop 1

DECIDING WHAT TO DO

I know from teaching that deciding what to do can be as problematic as how to do it. If you find yourself in this position, my suggestion is to sit down quietly with as many books and magazines as you can gather and pick out the images that really please you. Your local library will carry a wide range of books; try looking through those which illustrate the art and life-styles of different cultures. Set aside a number of appealing images, and then finally choose one as your starting point. From all the images you could have chosen, this selection is no small step on the way to developing a personal style. Another advantage to beginning in this way, is that the change from what may be a three-dimensional object to a two-dimensional one will have already been made for you. As you work, your likes and dislikes will take over and your own style will evolve.

Making pictures is all about pleasing yourself, but ideas don't come from thin air: the more you see, the more selective and sensitive to your own likes and dislikes you will become.

I hope you will make one or two pictures throughout the course of reading my book, perhaps even exploring many different ideas while working with me. I particularly enjoy creating pictures using timeless subjects. Combining my interpretation with those worked by people from different ages and cultures gives me great pleasure. The bird is one such image, and if you haven't already fixed on a subject, I suggest that your first picture be a bird. It allows for incorporating plenty of your own ideas and there is a huge variety of possible bird images to choose from. Why not start an inspiration pinboard by collecting as many pictures of birds as you can find? You can pick elements from a number of bird images to make your own bird, or you may prefer to copy just one bird.

Drawing of a pinboard

CHAPTER 2

Fabrics

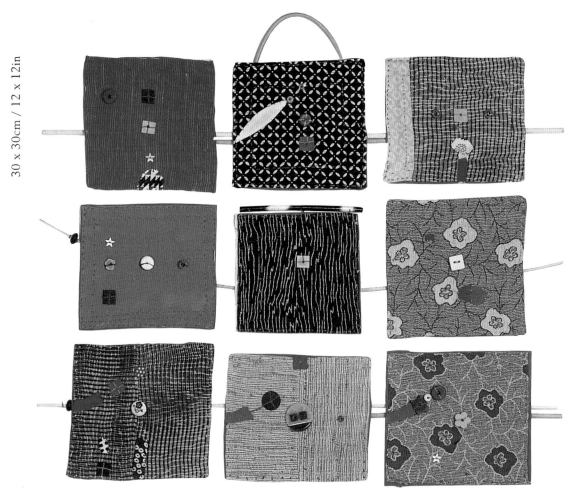

30 x 30cm / 12 x 12in

Japanese Pieces

Fabric is the mainstay of my work. You just can't have enough of it, but you don't need large quantities of any one fabric, because the scale that you will be working on is so small. Building up a fabric collection can be great fun. You never know where the hunt will lead - department stores, specialist fabric shops and soft furnishing stores for remnants and off-cuts; charity shops and jumble sales for such bits and pieces as ties, scarves and old clothes that can be bought for next to nothing. Look out for sample books and bags of scraps; these are often on sale in soft furnishing stores. Then, of course, fabric fanatics can buy new clothes with a second life in mind for them.

Swatches

Friends will join in, and their contributions can be a great challenge to your ingenuity. *Japanese Pieces* was inspired by a gift of scraps from old Japanese kimonos. This exciting bundle of fabrics contained an inspiring variety of textures, weaves, weights, colours and patterns. There were heavy, closely woven cottons and linens in deep indigo, rich plum colours and saturated reds and silk linings in brilliant bursts of pink, green, orange and red. So enchanting were these pieces that I couldn't resist cutting out small squares and playing about with them.

Silk Squares

In this pleasing and simple crib quilt from America, the fabric is the subject of the 'picture'. Like myself when making *Japanese Pieces*, the maker of this quilt felt inspired by the voice of her fabrics. She has arranged her small squares of silk into a simple grid pattern, fastening the three layers of the quilt with sharply contrasting black thread. The simplicity of the design allows the fabrics to speak for themselves.

Basket of American quilt scraps

The old American quilt pieces in the basket above, some dating back to the 1870s, were another gift from a fellow enthusiast I had met through my work. Fabric is such an evocative material, full of personal memories. The washed and worn quality of the old quilts reminded me of the sun-bleached clothing I wore on the beach as a child. From these fabrics, a new series of pictures followed. There is something very fulfilling in re-working materials that were originally made with another purpose in mind, and creating from them a new reality.

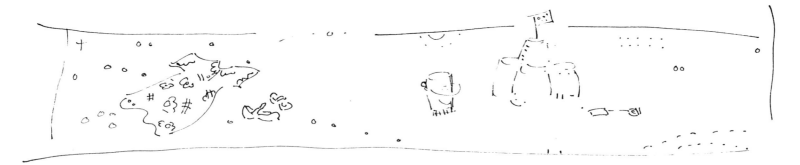

25 x 16.5cm / 10 x 6 ¹/₂in

Young Girl as Happy as a Sandboy

30.5 x 22.5cm / 12 x 9in

At the Seaside

Since there is such a wealth of fabric available, both old and new, enjoy the excitement of placing many diverse materials together. Remember that some fabrics have a distinct style and are easily recognizable. Their style can be so strong that any picture you make can be dominated by their distinctive character. It is preferable not to use fabrics from just one source as it usually makes for a bland picture, without accents and focus.

This dulling effect is also present in pictures I have started to make with fabrics that I have expressly dyed to use in one picture. Dyeing fabrics is a wonderful way of extending your palette – the more choice of colour and texture you have, the better – but use the newly dyed pieces sparingly.

My own dyeing methods are not very scientific. I use tea or onion skins and make the colour fast with salt. By crumpling the fabric before immersion in the dye pan, you can achieve different patterns and colour variations. The background for *Two Bees* is heavy cotton with an unusual wavy weave. The original cloth was white, before I dyed it with tea.

Don't be afraid of experimenting. Since you won't always know the composition of your fabrics and won't be able to follow exact dyeing instructions, put a selection of different fabrics and colours into your dye pan to see what happens. Try tie-dyeing or batik, the principle being to keep the dye away from some areas of the cloth. To tie-dye, fold or roll your cloth, then tie string tightly around it at different intervals, before dipping into dye. To batik, run hot wax onto your cloth randomly or make a pattern, before immersing it in cold water dyes. Commercial dyes can greatly extend your range of colours. Some can be used in a washing machine which allows you to dye many different fabrics at the same time. There are many techniques for dyeing fabrics and hundreds of recipes for making your own natural dyes. If you are interested in augmenting your fabric collection by dyeing fabrics, there are plenty of books and courses on the subject.

When collecting, remember to look for foundation fabrics as well as fabrics for the top shapes. Your picture will be built up from small, usually lightweight shapes arranged on a foundation fabric. The foundation can be quite heavy; a medium-weight furnishing fabric is suitable. It needs to be firm enough to handle when sewing the picture shapes on. The practical requirements also fulfil an aesthetic one. Pieces sewn to a ground that does not look

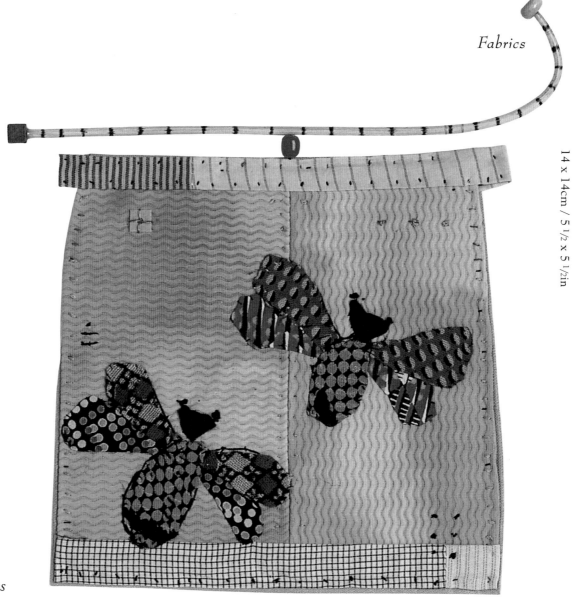

Two Bees

firm enough to hold their weight can also look unbalanced within the composition. This need for balance of foreground and background fabrics is also true when considering the top shapes. Heavy shapes on a flimsy ground will make for a very uneasy picture. If you find a fabric that is perfect in colour or weave for your foundation but too lightweight, lay it onto another piece of cloth and treat the two pieces as one. This simple solution allows for a greater freedom of choice.

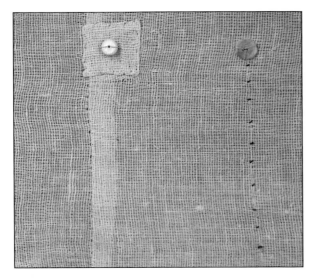

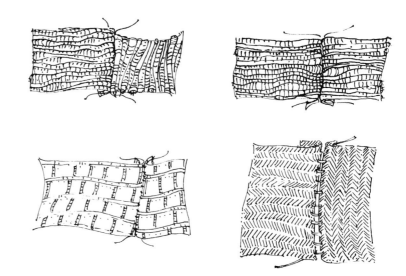

Detail of weave

Repositioning the weave of the fabric

Look for fabrics with interesting weaves. These can be cut and repositioned with the weave going in different directions. Many hand-woven fabrics have a distinct weave, the strands being woven loosely for the pattern to be noticeable. I particularly enjoy working on a foundation with a loose square weave, and get great satisfaction at the thought that the techniques I use to make my pictures mirror the materials I use. Weaving thread in and out with my needle to apply a shape is complementary to the manufacture of textiles.

25 x 6cm / 10 x 2 ¹/₂in

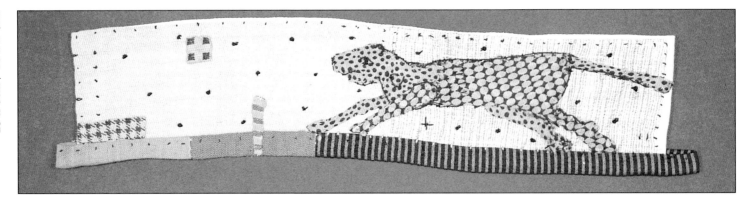

The Cheetah

When selecting fabrics for the top images, keep in mind that the raw edges will be turned under when the shape is sewn into place. This is difficult to do with any sensitivity if the fabric is too stiff or heavy. Cotton, lawn, fine wool, muslin, silk and lightweight linen are all suitable. Old, well-washed fabrics are ideal, as all the chemical size, which is responsible for the stiffness, has been removed. This makes them soft and easy to handle, and a small turning for a hem remains in place with gentle finger-pressing. If using new fabrics it is helpful to wash them a time or two before sewing. Polyester, nylon and synthetic fabrics of all kinds can be 'springy' and harder to control when sewing. These fabrics may not be to your taste but they can offer a palette of vivid colours which could be just what is needed to enliven your picture, if used sparingly.

Making pictures on this scale uses the smallest of fabric scraps. But this doesn't mean that you should only be looking for small-scale prints. In fact, placing a complete motif such as a small flower can be difficult. The eye recognizes the shape and is drawn to it, giving it more importance than the image you have made. This can spoil the balance and composition of your picture. Don't ignore fabrics with a large-scale pattern. Cutting across shapes can give some very useful combinations of line and colour.

If you are working from a photograph or picture do not restrict yourself to searching for exact colour and pattern matches for each separate element. Look for appropriate colours, of course, but then study your fabrics to see how the colours affect each other. Watch how one colour can diminish another one, yet make a different colour sing out and glow.

You as the creator have complete control and freedom to change colours. Use your inspiration as a starting point only, then let the picture you are making take over. This will help you compose with what is to hand and will help curb the temptation to include certain fabrics because they seem so absolutely appropriate. Finding a fabric that has a feather pattern and is exactly the colour of the bird that you are recreating does not mean that it is necessarily the right choice for your picture. A slightly different colour might work much better in the reality of your picture and the feather pattern may dominate the entire composition. Even when working with paint, where you are able to mix exact colours, colour choices are made and altered to suit personal requirements, rather than to produce slavish copies of the real thing.

Workshop 2

FABRICS

Birds in different fabrics

1. Start your own collection of fabrics.

2. Gather together suitable fabrics to make a bird picture. Keep in mind the different qualities needed for the foundation and the top shapes.

3. I started the quilt shown on page 37 many years ago, with the idea of incorporating all the pieces of fabric I had. This simple and rewarding exercise offers a marvellous opportunity to understand the nature of fabrics. I would heartily recommend it to those of you who have not had a lot of experience handling fabrics. I used the traditional English patchwork technique of folding fabric around a paper template and then joining the shapes together. It is also great fun to see just how many incredibly diverse patterns and colours can be held together by the simple device of contrasting lines of light and dark. As you look at your growing quilt, memories will flood back. Twenty years later I can still remember exactly where all the scraps came from.

Triangle Quilt

CHAPTER THREE

Foundation ~ Preparing Your Ground

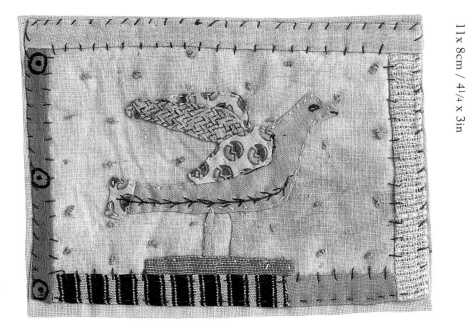

11x 8cm / 4¼ x 3in

The Small Bird

The foundation is the background on which your picture is built. Select a suitable-coloured fabric, keeping in mind that the background fabric needs to be heavy enough to hold all the top (appliqué) shapes, then decide on the size that will best suit your picture. You may instinctively prefer to work on either a large or a small scale. Remember that as this work is mainly hand-stitched, a large picture may take a long time to complete. I prefer to work on a small scale, which takes less stitching time and allows me to explore one theme through many pictures. *The Bird and the Tiger* is about as large as I like to work, and *The Small Bird* and *An Enclosed Garden* are as small. Any smaller, and manipulating the fabric is too awkward to be enjoyable.

60 x 60cm / 24 x 24in

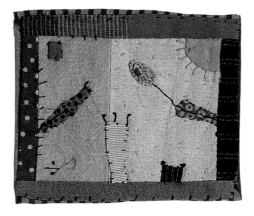

9 x 8cm / 3 ½ x 3 ¼in

ABOVE: *An Enclosed Garden*

LFFT: *The Bird and the Tiger*

Another point to consider when selecting the foundation is the format you want your picture to be. I have found that many people have strong preferences for working on either a landscape shape (wider than high), or portrait shape (higher than wide). It is helpful to be pleased with the basic shape of the picture before you add any picture images.

A subject may dictate the format of the foundation. When deciding on the shape of the foundation for *Garden for a Sacred Cow*, my thought was to create a fitting ambience in which to place the image of the Indian cow. I chose to use two tapered rectangles reminiscent

39

23 x 23cm / 9 x 9in

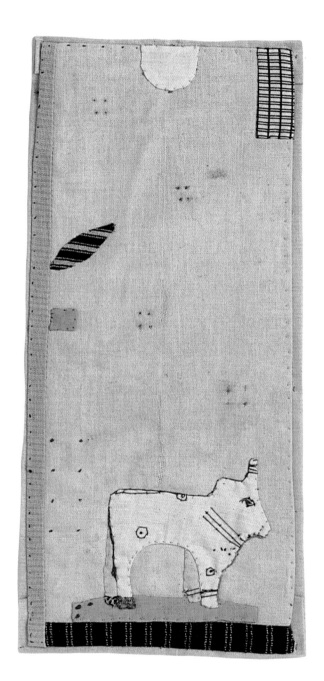
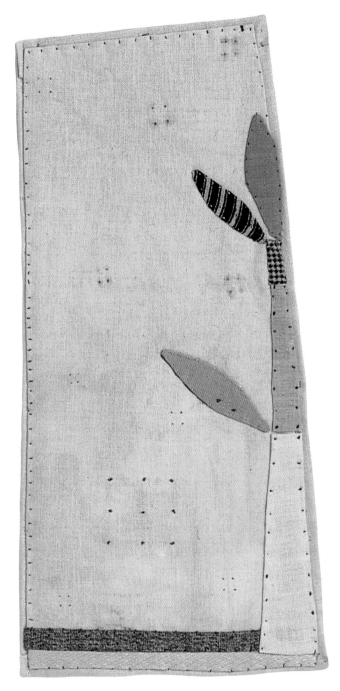

Garden for a Sacred Cow

of blocks of hewn stone, suggesting the remains of something monumental, perhaps the entrance to an ancient temple. Here the idea of the subject dictated the shape of the foundation.

In other cases, the shape of the applied image governs the shape used for the foundation. For example, a tall vase of flowers will probably look most comfortable on a portrait shape, but equally could be placed on a square or a landscape-shaped background to great effect. The variations are endless, and it is worth looking at many pictures and noting how a subject occupies its foundation. Some subjects cover most of the background, while others sit sparsely in a lot of open space. Don't be afraid of empty spaces – they are as important as the shapes applied.

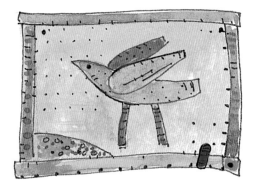

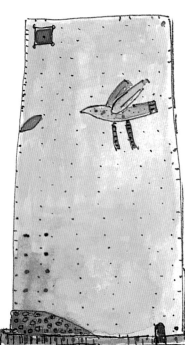

Format variations

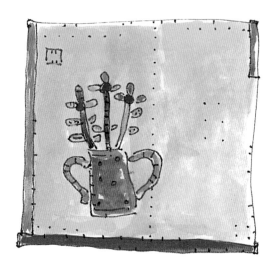

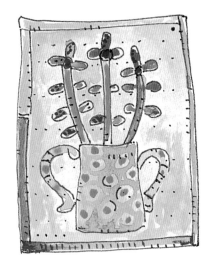

As your picture develops, you might find the foundation too small or the wrong shape, and want to change either the dimensions or format, or both. This can be easily achieved with fabric. The initial shape can be built up from several separate backgrounds or added to indefinitely by simply sewing on another piece of fabric. *Girls at the Seaside* started off as a rectangle, and then the idea of describing the beach as a wide open space, stretching away, dominated my thoughts, so I extended the foundation at the base only with an additional border. This solution brought with it an unexpected bonus: the extra seamline created a new dimension to the work, giving the picture the break between sea and sand.

Girls at the Seaside

The picture *Reflections in a Square Pond* began life as two fish on a small rectangle of fabric. When laying wavy lines of cotton thread on top of the fish to suggest water currents, I realized that the foundation was too small and that the water currents seemed to stop mid-flow. I solved the problem of a too-small pond by placing the picture on a larger, rectangular foundation, eventually progressing to a third and larger pond. Even the title of the piece

40 x 15cm / 16 x 6in

derives from this simple development of an ever-increasing background shape. The three backgrounds, one on top of the other, remind me of the reflections of buildings on still water.

Similarly, *Hens in the Farmyard* was originally intended to remain within one rectangle. On completing the work I found that, like the fish, they needed more space. Not having a larger piece of the same background fabric, I explored various alternatives, such as placing the picture on other fabrics. The freedom and ease with which your 'canvas' can be changed as a new idea develops is one of the great joys of working with fabric. It is also one of its challenges. Searching for a sympathetic fabric to replace one that you have just run out of can be invigorating and may suggest many exciting new choices to pursue.

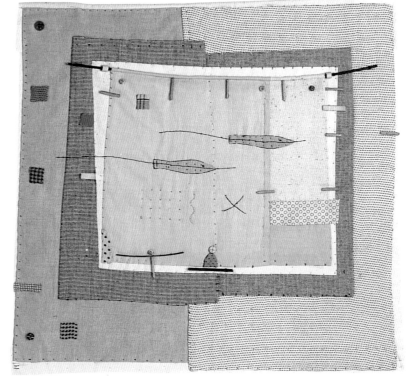

47 x 42cm / 18 ¹/₂ x 16 ¹/₂in

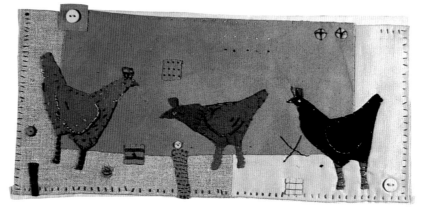

25 x 14cm / 10 x 5 ¹/₂in

TOP RIGHT: *Reflections in a Square Pond*
BOTTOM RIGHT: *Hens in the Farmyard*

43

Before finally deciding on your background fabric, spend some time playing with the range of fabrics that you have in mind for the top shapes. Lay the small pieces onto as many different backgrounds as you can find. Neutral-coloured backgrounds, or very dark grounds against which other colours glow, serve me best. The foundation of *The Small Bird* at the beginning of the chapter is a tea-dyed calico.

Once you have decided on your background fabric, press it well and lay it onto a heavy, plain white or cream-coloured card, large enough to leave a generous margin all the way around. This is an extremely useful device, and one that I couldn't work without. As you work, you will end up with all sorts of distracting bits and pieces around you. Your portable planning board allows you to isolate your work so that you can 'see' what is happening within your picture. It provides a clear and defined space in which to arrange and rearrange your shapes.

Planning board

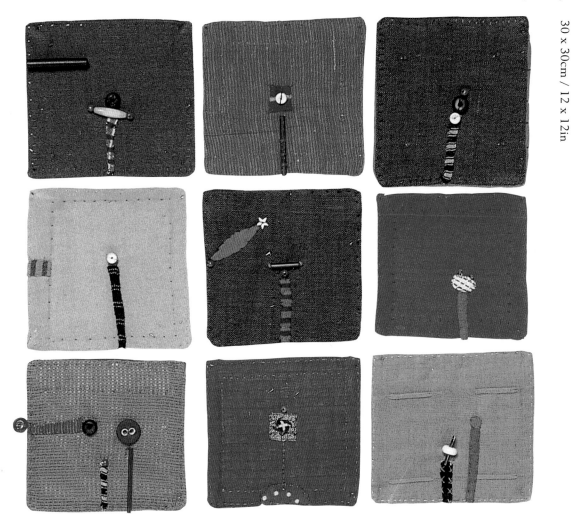

30 x 30cm / 12 x 12in

Seedlings Spaced with Special Care

Seedlings Spaced with Special Care is one picture that developed as a direct result of working with this technique. Inspired by the neat squares of experimental plant beds, each with one or two seeds, I arranged a series of small squares on my planning board. My intention was to join the squares into a single unit. I realized that in the process of arranging the fabrics I was enjoying glimpses of white between the squares, and decided to incorporate this second grid as part of my interpretation.

Looking through the book you will notice that some of my pictures have borders. After preparing my background fabric I often make a fabric border, and compose a picture to fit. A border can be added later, after the picture is in place. However, most beginners find a foundation framed with a border a helpful device when building up a composition.

Finding a suitable border

At this stage, I would normally sew a backing cloth to the foundation. It has several functions. It offers extra stability to your picture and may be essential if you have chosen to use a particularly lightweight foundation. It conceals seams and it provides a base on which to sew the foundation. I generally use curtain lining or a similar weight fabric.

You can choose to make the backing cloth visible from the front, and thus an important part of your picture. The thin, framing line of the backing cloth can provide that small detail of colour which will hold the whole composition together. A sharp colour or a tonal contrast can add sparkle to a quiet picture. A neutral colour can tone down and help hold in place a multicoloured piece. In *Seedlings Spaced with Special Care* you can see that each square is placed on a carefully chosen backing cloth. The small flashes of colour provide just the right degree of contrast and framing to ensure that the delicate seedlings remain protected and separate. It would have been a rather bland picture without this extra touch of colour.

Workshop 3

FOUNDATION ~ PREPARING YOUR GROUND

Having chosen your subject and selected suitable fabrics, it is time to prepare your foundation. The following illustrations show you, in step-by-step fashion, how to prepare your ground and make borders, and how the foundation is attached to the backing cloth. The last illustration shows a backing cloth left visible from the front. If this extra definition is not required, simply turn in the raw edge of the backing cloth a little further. Remember to add a 0.6cm / $^1/_4$ in seam allowance as you cut out all the pieces.

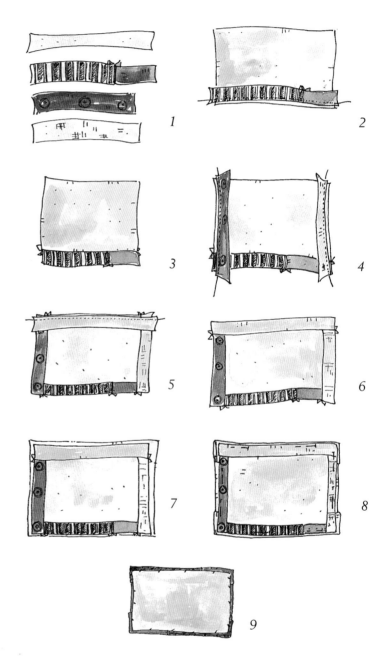

CHAPTER FOUR

Cutting Shapes to Compose With

15 x 10cm / 6 x 4in

Two Balloons Floating Along

Having chosen a background and a good selection of fabrics, the next step is to cut out the shapes to make up your picture. In conventional appliqué, the cut-out shape is a larger version of the final shape. The shapes are then pinned in place, and the raw edges turned under and sewn down. In contrast, I prefer to cut out my shapes to the finished size with no turning-under allowance. I use these as compositional shapes only. To see and evaluate the shapes in your picture clearly, it is important to compose with shapes cut to their finished size. If you make a picture where all the shapes have been cut to include a turning-under allowance, it is impossible to arrange them with any certainty or sensitivity. Many of the shapes will overlap, the spaces between the shapes will be obscured and you will end up with quite an incorrect reading of your final picture. When I am happy with the arrangement of shapes, I replace them with larger shapes of the same fabric. I add an extra 0.6cm / $^1/4$ inch all around the shape to allow for turning under.

Make sure that you have a sharp pair of scissors. There is nothing more frustrating than trying to chew through cloth with blunt scissors, and there is something so satisfying about working with a good sharp pair. The crispness of the cut, the accuracy you can achieve, and the wonderful 'crunching' noise they make as they cut into fabric makes it so worthwhile to invest in a good pair, setting them aside to be used for cutting fabric exclusively.

I visualize the shape I want, and then cut it out freehand, holding the cloth in my hand and moving it as I cut. Don't be afraid to use this method. You used it with supreme confidence as a child. Try cutting your shapes against a plain background. It is easier to see the shape being made. If necessary you can refine your shape by placing it on your planning board. Hold it down with a fingertip, pick up the edge that needs adjustment with the blade of your scissors, and cut to shape.

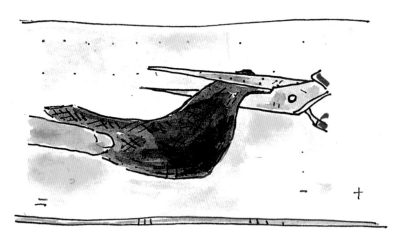

Taking a fraction more off the beak

Many people find it reassuring to make a cardboard template first, and then to trace the shape onto the fabric before cutting. This is not necessary for simple shapes such as a petal or stem, but it might be helpful for the more complicated shapes of animals and birds. For those of you who have no confidence in your drawing skills, I have provided several templates at the end of the book. You can always cut out an image from a magazine and use it as a template.

To make a re-usable template, trace your shape onto heavy card and cut out. Place the template on the right side of your fabric and trace around the shape with a sharp pencil. To reverse the image, simply place your template face down on the fabric.

Most images will be a mixture of curves and straight lines. When using curved shapes in your picture, cut the fabric on the bias, that is, across the weave. Fabric cut this way has more stretch and can be shaped into smooth curves.

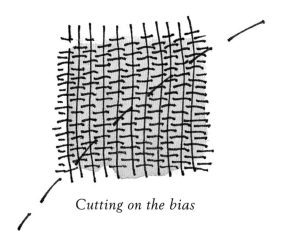

Cutting on the bias

One last point: look at the next four pictures and you will notice that some shapes were cut as a single shape and others were made up of separately cut shapes. Creating an image from several separate shapes allows you greater freedom to introduce changes in colour, texture and placement. It is also possible to define sharp angles if the image is made up of a number of separate shapes.

23 x 18cm / 9 x 7in

The African Goose

20 x 10cm / 8 x 4in

This Year's Lamb

10 x 7.5cm / 4 x 3in

Two Bears

12.5 x 9cm / 5 x 3¹/₂in

The Elephant

Workshop 4

CUTTING OUT COMPOSITIONAL SHAPES

20 x 12cm / 8 x 5in

Sheep in the making

Note: All the shapes that you are cutting out for this workshop will be compositional shapes or shapes cut to the finished size, without a turning-under allowance.

1. Press your fabrics well before you cut. Creases spoil the line and prevent the fabric from lying flat.

2. If making a bird picture, cut out some simple bird shapes, using a template, then cut some freehand. Try to cut holding the shape against a board. I find it makes such a difference – you can really 'see' the shape emerging.

3. Cut a variety of simple wing shapes ready to place in different positions.

4. Experiment with cutting shapes from very different materials.

5. Cut out some of the birds with the legs attached, and cut some as separate shapes.

6. Cut out some flower and leaf shapes.

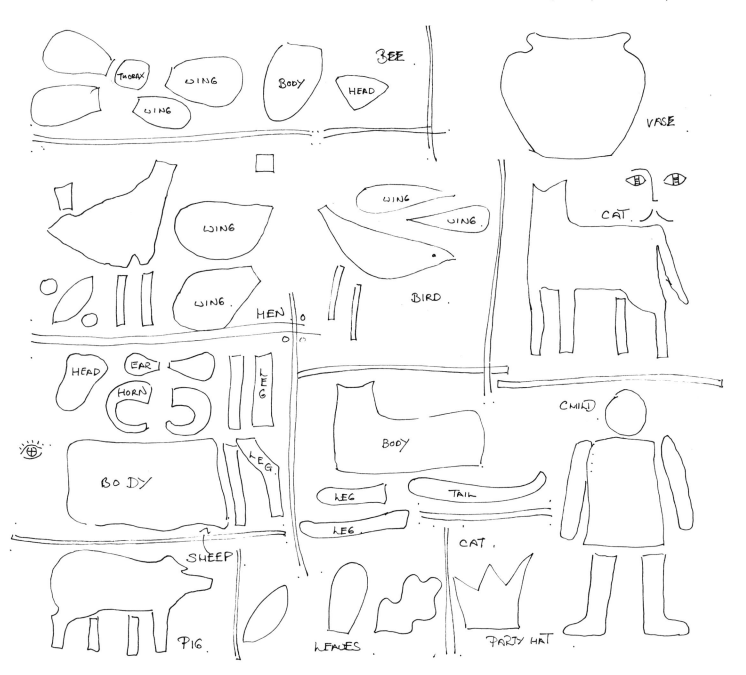

Drawings of prepared pieces

CHAPTER FIVE

Composition ~ Arranging Your Shapes

28 x 9cm / 9 x 3 ¹/₂in

Black Cat Surveying All

Making a composition is simply a matter of arranging all the elements of your picture into a harmonious whole, to create both mood and an arresting pattern of shape and colour. You make spatial decisions all the time – hanging a picture, arranging ornaments, for instance. And we have all experienced the great satisfaction when a new piece of furniture fits as if it were designed for the room, and the irritation when it doesn't. In picture making, life is a lot easier; if an element doesn't fit you simply move the walls! Deciding on your composition is absorbing, exciting work and you should never be daunted by the immensity of your options. Remember, whatever you create need only please you.

The placement of what you decide to include and what you choose to leave out gives your picture its voice. A composition can be sad, witty, humorous, quiet or busy; it can effect any number of emotional responses. Many small shapes and colours all crowded together in a haphazard way can create a feeling of confusion and busyness, while shapes placed on a grid formation remain calm and steady.

Your composition is not just made up of applied shapes. In the excitement of arranging all your pieces and concentrating on them, it can be all too easy to forget the impact of the shapes left between. I chose *Black Cat Surveying All* to illustrate the importance of these abstract shapes. In themselves they don't make a recognizable image but they can convey an atmosphere and create a mood. Jagged, pointed shapes can look aggressive, uncomfortable and angry, while horizontal shapes with soft, gentle curves can evoke a sense of calm tranquillity. As it is the interlocking of shapes that pleases me, I tend to keep my compositions uncrowded. In *Black Cat Surveying All*, you can see that the shapes in between the cat and the borders, and the negative shapes made by the position of the flowers and sun, are just as strong and clearly defined as the picture shapes.

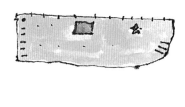

Shapes in between

By making simple shapes, each having plenty of space around it, I was hoping to emphasize the aloofness of the cat and at the same time create a calm and steady picture. Another alternative would have been to place the cat against many, small shapes and by contrast draw attention to its aloofness. However, pursuing this path would have made the overall mood of the picture one of agitation and restlessness.

I used the flowers to suggest a garden stretching out towards the viewer. They also provided me with an excuse to interrupt the bottom border and create a pleasing pattern. The tail breaking out of the picture was positioned to give the cat its freedom, and I used the flower coming in from the opposite side to balance the strong directional movement. To secure the powerful shape of the cat, its legs were planted firmly onto the bottom border.

8.5 x 12.5cm / 3 ¹/₂ x 6in

Two Flowers

Tempting as it is to start sewing, don't rush – give yourself time. You will probably spend more time on this stage than on any other. I am often asked how long it takes to make a picture. This is an impossible question to answer, and of very little importance. A small simple composition such as *Two Flowers* did take much longer to complete than some larger pieces made up of many more elements.

Sometimes your picture falls into place quickly and easily, but often you can arrange and rearrange and nothing seems right. When this happens, put the picture away and do something else; there is no fun struggling on and on. Also, when you work on the same piece for too long it is very easy to stop 'seeing'. This is perfect work for people with a busy day as a moment snatched for a quick look can be very productive. It will often give you a new perspective even if you can't do anything about it there and then. Nothing will dry up or become unusable; the pieces are awaiting your return. I always work on several pictures at the same time, moving from one to another to see each with a fresh eye.

Behind Our Back Garden

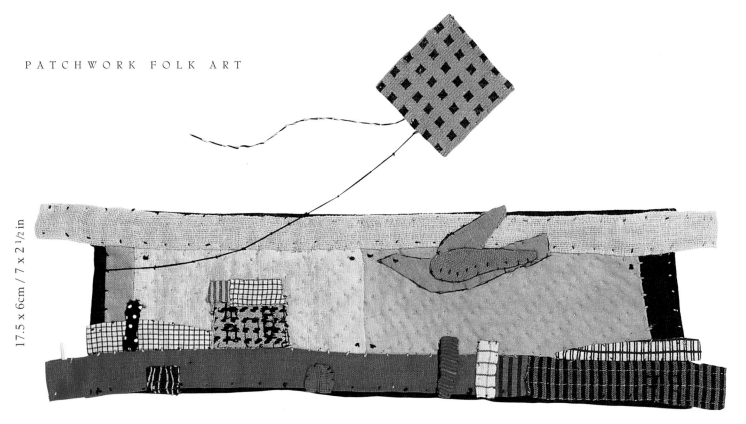

17.5 x 6cm / 7 x 2 ½ in

Kite Above the Yellow Bird

Working around themes has real advantages, for as you are arranging your composition many possibilities will present themselves, and the temptation is to try to put them all in the same picture. This can make your work too complicated and overcrowded. If you are working on a number of pictures within one theme, it leaves you relaxed knowing that you will probably find a home for all your ideas. With many ideas in store, your work will develop in a purposeful way.

An awareness of tonal contrast (how light or dark a colour can be) can help you in arranging your composition. Blue, yellow, green and red can sit happily side by side, commanding the same attention, if they are similar in tone.

By manipulating tonal contrast you can also give depth to your picture. A picture with little tonal contrast, for instance *Barn on the Moors* in Chapter 1, will result in a very flat work. To make your picture appear to be a 'window in the wall', choose colours for your foreground shapes that provide a strong tonal contrast to the background. To create a sense of things receding in the distance, gradually reduce the tonal contrast between the objects.

Half shut your eyes and look at the vase of flowers. The flowers, although a variety of colours, all stand out from the dark background. If they had all been the same colour but very different in tone, it would have been an unsuccessful picture. Some details would have stood out, and others would have receded, giving the picture a livelier but jumpy feeling – a far cry from the calm, and timeless quality I was trying to create.

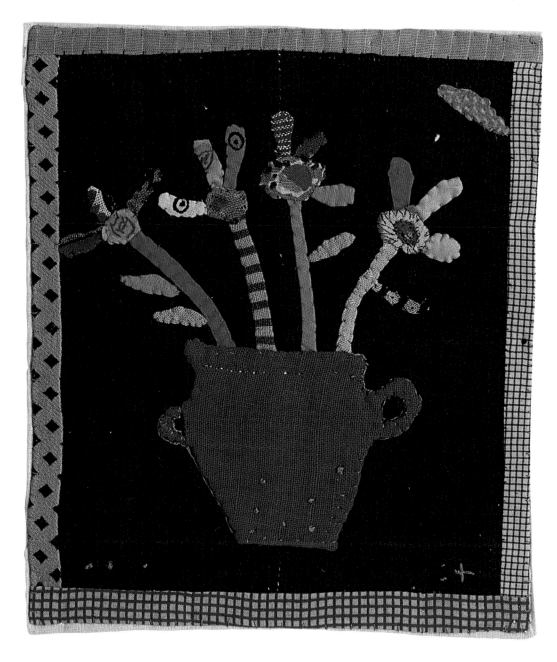

15 x 16cm / 6 x 6 ¹/₂in

The Vase

12.5 x 10cm / 5 x 4in

Two Hares Listening

The picture shown above, with its oversized hares in a small frame, works because of the tonal balance of colours. By the same token, the tonal similarity of colours in *The Lighthouse* helps unify a composition of many disparate borders and little block shapes.

25 x 10cm / 10 x 4in

The Lighthouse

Tonal balance, abstract shapes, and colour are simply tools to use, to be aware of when making your own picture. My last intention in writing this book is to set out any hard-and-fast rules, and thereby diminish the idiosyncrasies of another person's picture. Unique and personal visions must be within all of us. We can never really explain why some shapes and colour combinations please one person and not another. Some enjoy the firmness of a symmetrical grid foundation, others the swirling confusion of curve upon curve. Personal memories, character, shared human experience must all come into play.

The texture and weave of your fabric can have a bearing on your composition.

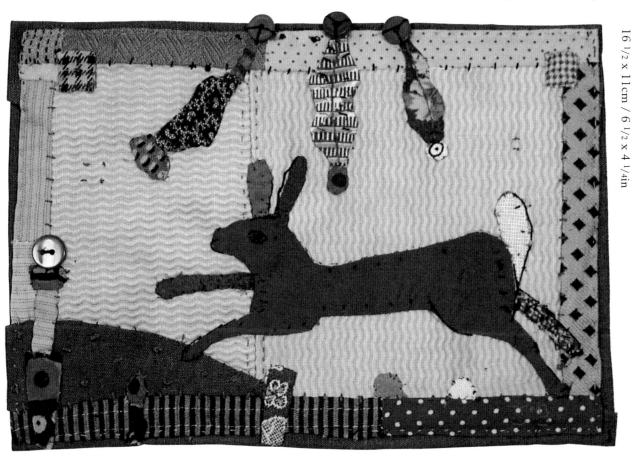

16 ½ x 11cm / 6 ½ x 4 ¼in

Brown Hare Leaping

Whilst working on *Hens in the Fields* I wanted to create a sense of the fields in which the hens might wander. The foundation fabric I had chosen had a pronounced wavy line in the weave, and so by simply cutting it into three pieces and repositioning them to alter the direction of the weave I was able to suggest a jigsaw pattern of interlocking fields. Using French seams I added further depth suggestive of changes in the terrain.

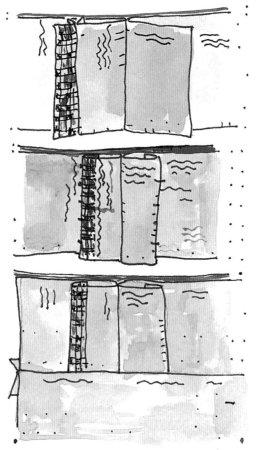

1. *Seam allowance left on right side of fabric.*

2. *Seam allowance turned under and sewn into place.*

3. *Large area attached by sewing over the French seam.*

Making a French seam

My foundation was very solid and imposing, so I had to be careful to find the right weight for the picture elements. I chose robust and bold shapes for the hens, and with the dome and rectangle at the very bottom of the picture I had just enough weight to counterbalance the heavy top half of the picture.

20 x 20cm / 8 x 8in

Hens in the Fields

65

Dragonflies each 9 x 11cm/3 1/2 x 4 1/2in

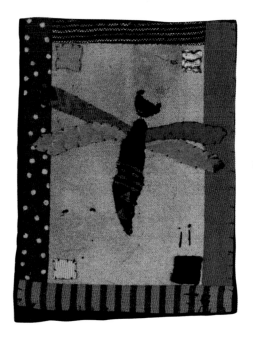 

Dragonflies

Exploring a composition doesn't stop until your picture is framed and hung. When making *Dragonflies*, I used the placement of the wings, head and body to suggest the gentle, smooth movement of flight. The contrast provided by the rigid framing and small, symmetrically placed squares helped me with the sense of movement I was trying to achieve. On finishing the picture, I decided to make a second picture to place beside the first. I felt that by reiterating the gentle curves, the eye would be carried from one picture to the next, in the same darting manner as the flight of a dragonfly.

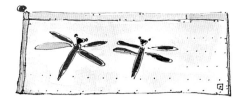 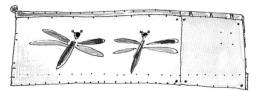 

Variations on a theme

12 x 6.5cm and 10 x 5cm / 4 ³/₄ x 2 ¹/₂in and 4 x 2 in

Two Angels Gliding By

Two Angels Gliding By started off as two separate pictures. By chance, I saw them side by side and realized that compositionally they were stronger as a pair, despite the differences between them.

Workshop 5

COMPOSITION ~ ARRANGING YOUR SHAPES

Arranging the bird shapes

You may have a good collection of bird shapes cut out and ready to arrange on your foundation (see page 36). Don't forget to place your picture on a planning board so that you can 'see' it clearly.

It is important to take your time and give yourself a chance to note all the differences even a slight repositioning can make. Fabric will usually hold to other fabric so it isn't necessary to pin down the pieces. This allows for such an enjoyable and direct way of working. Try finishing one arrangement and putting it away for a day. When you come back to it you may notice aspects that had previously slipped your attention.

19 x 6.5cm / 7 $^1\!/_2$ x 2 $^1\!/_2$in

Making One Bee, One Hive

One Bee, One Hive shows a work in progress, trying a number of different shapes, colours and positions before deciding on the final composition.

69

CHAPTER SIX

Turning Under ~ Drawing with Your Needle

16 x 17cm / 6 1/2 x 6 3/4in

Two Hens

By now the main elements of your picture will be in place but that does not exclude the possibility of incorporating new ideas, making small refinements, or even embarking on larger changes. From arranging your shapes you will be aware of how the slightest rearrangement can significantly alter the appearance and mood of a composition. This is particularly so in the turning-under process, as it is at this stage that your images will take on their final shape.

The following illustrations describe the technique of 'drawing' with a needle and sewing a shape to the foundation. The technique involves manipulating the raw edge of the fabric under with your needle to make a shape, and then securing it down with small, 'invisible' stitches.

Decide which element of your picture you will sew down first. I usually start with the main image. Remember to remove your compositional shapes first, and replace them with shapes of the same fabric, cut larger to allow for turning under. Give yourself a 0.6 cm / ¹/4 inch seam allowance at least. It is easy to snip a little more off once the edge has been finger-pressed under, but it is difficult to turn a very small edge. Also, some fabrics do not stay in place as well as others.

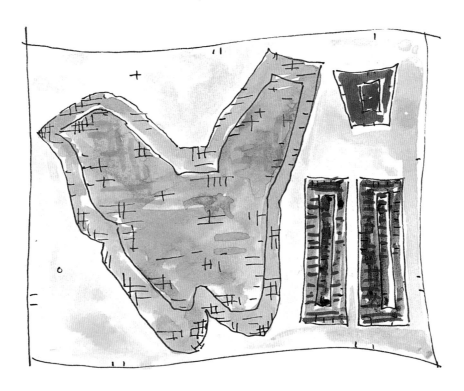

1. Remove the compositional guideline shapes and cut another set larger by 0.6 cm / ¹/4 inch all the way around. This will be your turning-under allowance.

2. Following your pre-planned composition, pin the 'new' shapes in place.

3. To sew your shape to the foundation, start by selecting as straight an edge as you can and secure the shape with two tiny stitches, one on top of the other. Define the shape of your image by easing the fabric under with your needle, and sew in position by bringing the needle up through the foundation and catching a few threads of the folded edge of the shape. Insert the needle back down into the foundation a fraction beyond the spot where it came up. As you sew, stop and look at the shape after every two or three stitches, and decide how to continue.

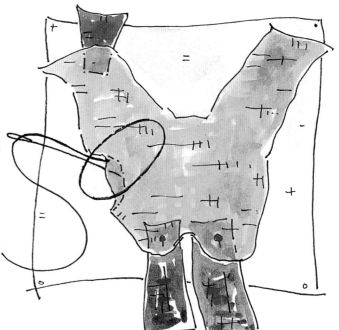

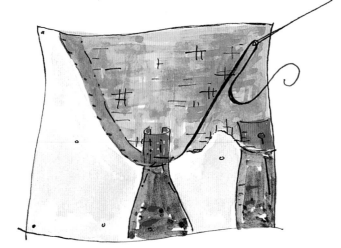

4. Catching the leg, turned under, before sewing across.

5. Turning the tail. Pushing the top fabric under.

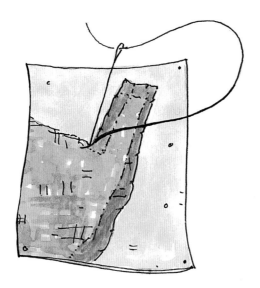

6. Choosing to make a larger or smaller indentation.

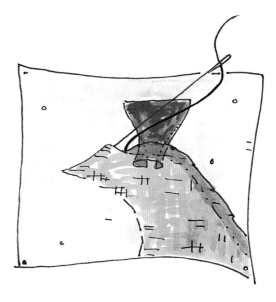

7. Sewing across the comb.

8. Pushing the fabric under at the neck indentation.

9.   After completing the body you can return to finish the legs and the comb.
Although you have already decided upon the approximate position of the legs you may
now want to make further adjustments. For instance, you may want to change a
straight leg to one with a slight curve. This is still possible even with the legs partially
sewn down. Fabric is yielding and can easily be adjusted and moved.

 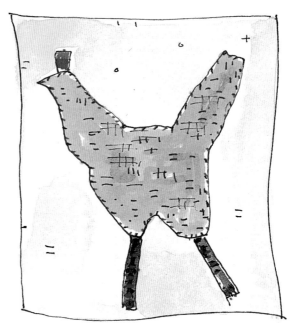

If fabric puckers when turning under, make a small snip at right angles to the sewn
line. This will release any tension. I find that when working with lightweight fabrics on
this scale, clipping is seldom necessary. When sewing down your shapes you will appreciate the ease with which fabric that has been cut on the bias can be turned under,
making it easy to produce curved shapes.

Having sewn one shape down, you now have the opportunity to readjust the position of the remaining shapes. Working with fabric you can draw and compose to the
very last stitch. Even at this stage you can still decide to take away some of the com-
ponents, or add others. Keep your mind open, and don't be afraid to move away from
your original intention if the picture is suggesting a change of direction.

12.5 x 12.5cm / 5 x 5in

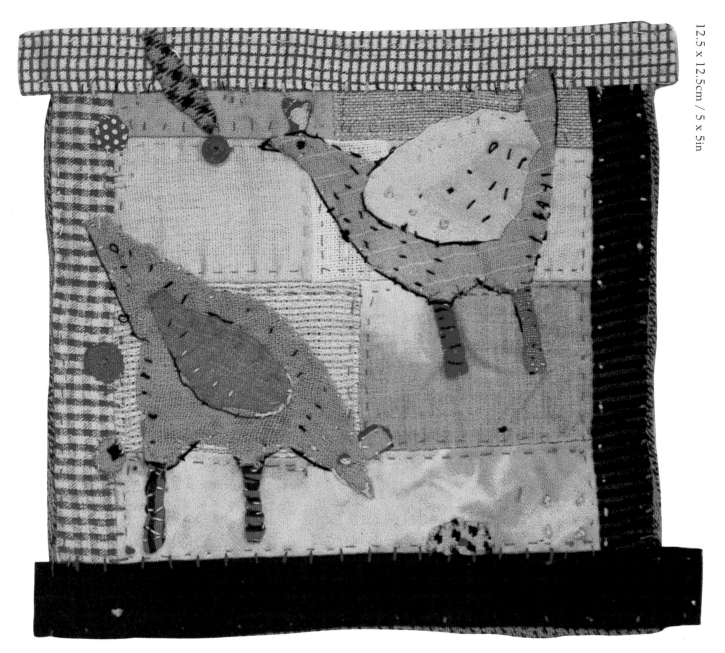

Two Brown Hens

20.5 x 20.5cm / 8 x 8in

The Hen Coop

76

Workshop 6

BLUE BIRD IN THE EARLY MORNING

23 x 9cm / 9 x 3 1/2in

Making Blue Bird in the Early Morning

1. Remove the compositional shapes from your bird picture and replace them with shapes cut to include a turning-under allowance.

2. Pin, then sew the new shapes in place. Where pieces overlap, stitch the underneath pieces to the foundation first. In most cases, it is best to work upwards, from background to foreground. Do not turn under edges that will be covered by other shapes.

I designed this *Flower Sampler* as a simple way of giving varied sewing and 'drawing' experience within one picture. It incorporates all the simple techniques you will ever need, no matter how complicated a picture you decide to make.

Flower Sampler

Flower A   All the petals have curved edges. Choose a wide range of fabrics, including silks, polyesters and cottons, to give you experience of their different qualities. Try cutting some straight across the fabric and others on the bias.

Flower B   All the petals have straight edges. Again, choose different fabrics but practise turning under sharp corners.

Flower C   A circular flower made by layering fabric. This will give you experience of how bulky work can become. You can then decide whether you like this padded quality and whether it would be appropriate for another picture.

Stems   Cut one stem on the bias, the other straight across the fabric, and try to curve both. You will notice a remarkable difference. The bias-cut fabric will give you elegant curves, while the straight-cut fabric will be much more difficult to manipulate.

CHAPTER SEVEN

Stitches to Be Seen

24 x 18cm / 9 1/2 x 7in

Ballooning over the Hill

In this chapter you'll discover how the simplest of 'added' stitches can transform a picture. A stitch can be placed with the same accuracy as a line drawn with a pen or pencil and can be used in the same precise way to add emphasis and interest. You'll be making stitches with deliberate accuracy but it won't be tedious as you won't be repeating the exact same stitch, over and over again. And if you don't like the stitch you have made, don't worry, fabric is forgiving and the stitch can be removed. By slightly manipulating the weave, the tiny hole left will disappear. With this security you can experiment with different stitches.

Finally, it is not necessary to be familiar with a comprehensive range of embroidery stitches. Since a stitch is an expressive line or 'mark', it can be totally your own invention.

Here are a few diagrams to illustrate a range of stitches that can be used variously, time and time again, to great effect. The important consideration is what to put where.

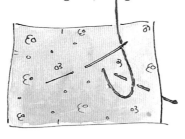

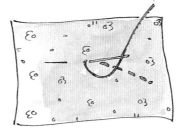

Backstitch
A backstitch makes a firmer indentation in the fabric and is useful when a series of dots or small lines is needed.

Running stitch

Backstitch

Overstitch
An overstitch is used for purely visual reasons, and added to pieces that have already been joined by machine or hand.

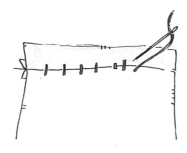

Overstitch

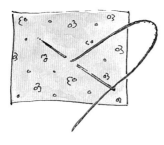

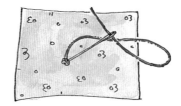

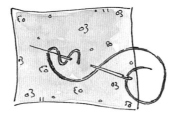

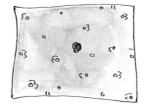

French knot

19 x 17cm / 7½ x 6½in

Two Runner Ducks

To illustrate how every 'mark' counts and how effective a few stitches can be, I have chosen two owl pictures. Their format is simple and there is little to compete for your attention. Look at the edges of the pictures and notice the variety of small black stitches; their irregularity attracts your attention and emphasizes the format. I did not want the seam joining the two different background fabrics to be

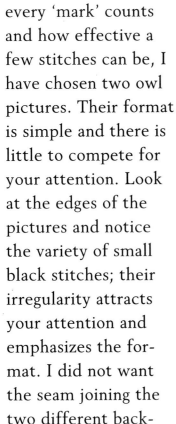

18 x 16.5cm / 7 x 6½in

Waiting for Night to Fall

noticeable, so I sewed it by machine. The regularity of the stitch is unassuming and withdraws from your notice. Also, machine sewing is speedy, and lets you get on with the more interesting aspects of the picture.

A stitched line can be as expressive as one made with a pencil. For instance, I chose to add to the edges of both owl pictures sturdy, almost straight stitches. These help to give a sense of calm and stillness. If I had been trying to create movement and lift for a different type of bird I would have used a series of exaggerated slanted stitches.

To suggest feathers I used a variety of stitches. At no time did I try to 'draw' the actual feather shape. Rather, I wanted to break up the surface texture with a suggestive and pleasing

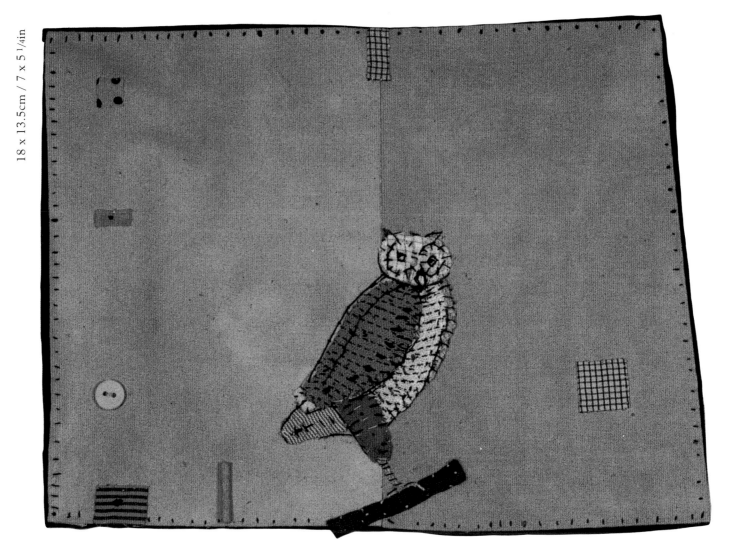

18 x 13.5cm / 7 x 5 ¹/₄in

At Dusk

pattern. You don't need to be too literal. Create an image that pleases you, even if it isn't true to life. If you look at the ropes on my balloon picture (*see page 79*) you will understand my mild disregard for accurate representation; the ropes going over my balloon wouldn't work in reality, and I certainly wouldn't like to fly in it, but the peculiar positioning of the ropes makes the image work for me.

To define the shape of the wing, which in colour is barely distinguishable from the background, I have used another extremely useful stitching technique called couching.

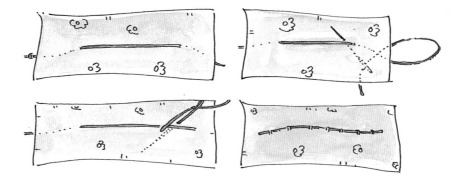

How to couch

As you can see, this really is using 'stitch as line'. The advantage of this versatile technique is that you can cut several pieces of thread and experiment with positions until you are happy with the result, and then secure them in place. You can use cotton sewing-machine thread for your couching lines. Double it if your picture requires a stronger line.

The flexibility of the couched line is ideal for creating trees.

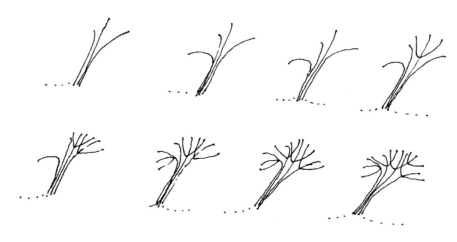

Stitching a tree

I also use this technique in my kite pictures to describe the movement of kite strings and tails, as well as the limbs of the kite flyers.

Stitching a limb

The children's bodies are made with small pieces of cloth but the movement and stances have been achieved by using a stitch as a drawn line.

The stitches used are so small they could remain in place without couching down the thread, or you could leave a little extra length to the stitch and couch the line at a bend, to describe a knee.

Detail

Variations on kite tails and children

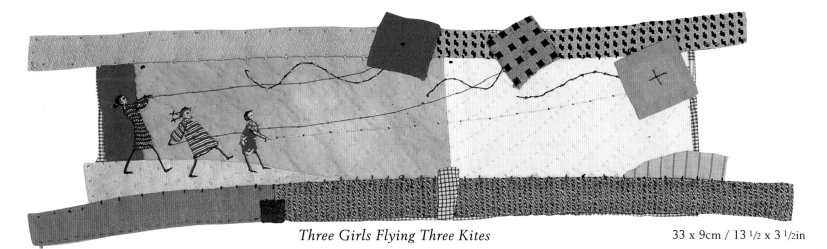

Three Girls Flying Three Kites   33 x 9cm / 13 1/2 x 3 1/2in

11 x 10cm / 4 1/2 x 3 3/4in

The Blue Party Hat

Making faces with stitches can be great fun. Try drawing a few faces on paper. You'll be surprised at what you can achieve with a few lines. The expression created is often unexpected – if it suits your requirement keep it. Many successful designs are happy 'accidents'. Try drawing faces on cloth with a fabric marking pen, and then sew over the lines. Soon you'll feel confident enough to 'draw' with your needle and thread.

Running Stitch

A running stitch (or quilting stitch) is just one way of creating a sense of movement in your picture. To suggest the wind currents in *Kite on a Cold and Windy Day*, I filled the large sky area with a running stitch. You will notice that the two background cloths have been quilted separately, the slight change suggesting varying gusts of wind.

I usually complete this type of stitching when the picture is in place and I can stitch through the various layers of fabric and into the backing cloth. The work is still sufficiently light and pliable to allow your needle to pick up four or five times before pulling the thread through. The tension depends on how defined and proud you want the stitching furrows to stand.

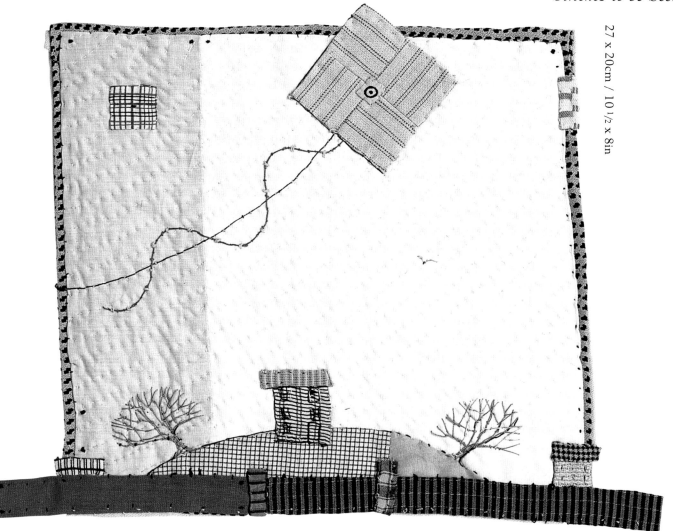

27 x 20cm / 10 ½ x 8in

Kite on a Cold and Windy Day

At this stage of your work, when using all-over stitching and when you are sewing through several layers of fabric, your stitching decisions are irreversible. Removing large areas will leave the fabric looking worn and damaged.

The couched lines making the trees were added after the running stitches were in place. If done the other way around, the movement of pulling the thread to the selected tension could pull the couched lines out of place.

Workshop 7

STITCHES TO BE SEEN

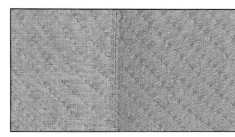

Detail of stitch lines

1. Practise making stitches of different size, tension and density in one small area of a piece of cotton fabric.

2. Try stitching on different weights of fabric.

3. Practise making stitching lines through several layers of fabric as if quilting. Do not attempt to imitate the precise stitch length and placement preferred by traditional quilters. Let your picture dictate the appearance of your stitches. It is worth noting that running stitches will naturally create curved lines. If your picture requires hard straight lines, you will need to put your work into a quilting hoop.

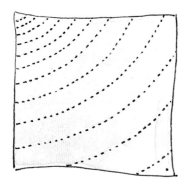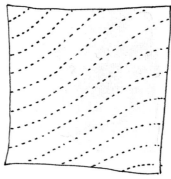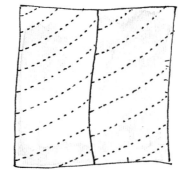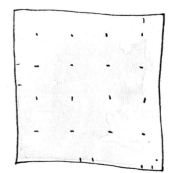

Varieties of stitch lines

4. Sew some simple fabric houses, and appliqué them to a plain background cloth. Use stitching to create the doors and windows.

Easy house shapes to piece and appliqué

You will realize just how few stitches are needed. The temptation is to add many stitch details and end up with an unwelcome density and focus. An indication is all that is needed. You don't have to fill in every window pane – let your 'mind's eye' do the rest.

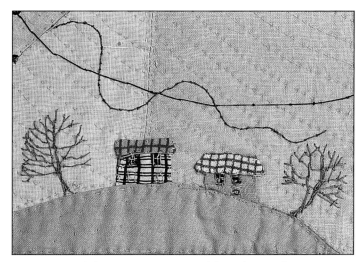

Detail from Kite on a Cold and Windy Day

5. Look carefully at the trees and try stitching several different shapes.

CHAPTER EIGHT

Added Objects

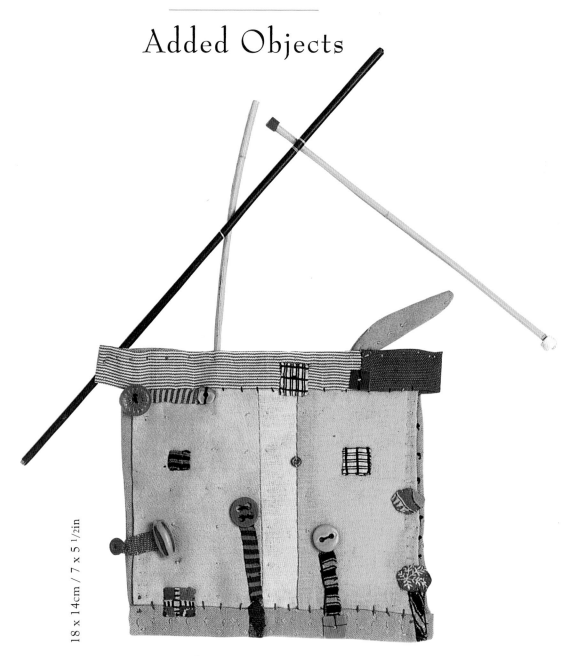

18 x 14cm / 7 x 5 1/2in

The Summer House

I delight in using 'found objects', or adding other non-fabric materials to my pictures, and making them an integral part of the composition. The contrast or similarity between materials can be used to give a new dimension to a picture. The difference between the shiny, light-reflective surface of a glass bead can emphasize the soft, light-absorbing qualities of a particular fabric. Bright touches catch the eye and draw the viewer's attention. The mottled surface of a bone bead can echo the variegated colours of a tea-dyed foundation, or the hard-edged quality of the bone can be used to create contrast and tension between the various fabrics used.

The pictures in this chapter show some of the ways in which added objects have become part of my work.

Objects associated with needlework are an obvious choice when working with fabric. But just because a button has a picture of a boat on it, or has been cut in the shape of a boat doesn't necessarily make it suitable for a seascape. The idea might seem right, but unless it is appropriate in colour, shape and texture it is best left out of your picture. Forcing an object to fit because you are so delighted with it can cause compositional problems.

11 x 11cm / 4¹/₂ x 4¹/₂in

The Christmas Hare before and after sequins

The Christmas Hare is a bright image leaping out against a dark background. When working on the picture I knew that I needed to find a visual link between the hare and the background to hold the hare in place. I had planned to use white French knots but they weren't strong enough and became lost in the snow! A scattering of sequins provided the balance my picture needed, as well as stars for the night sky. Although I enjoyed seeing the play of light and dark in the reflective sequins, I was concerned that it might be distracting, and draw focus away from the subject. As it turned out the hare was bold enough to hold its own.

Basket cane is another favourite material of mine. It is very adaptable and is sympathetic to fabric. It can be bought in different thicknesses from department stores and craft shops. It can be cut, split, painted, sewn through or over to hold it in place, and is flexible enough to shape into curves, without soaking in water first.

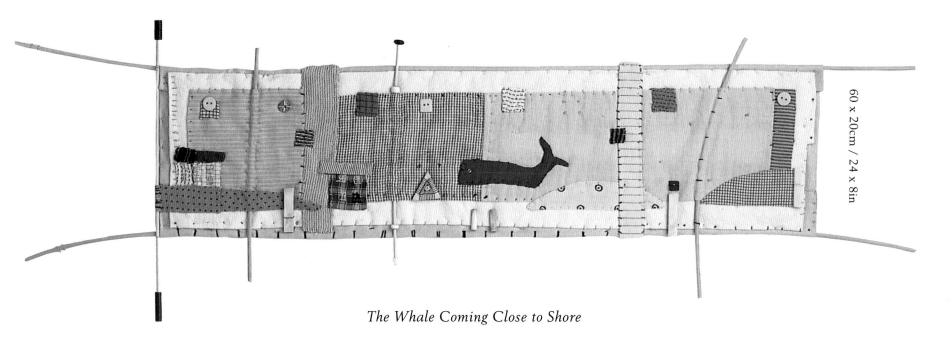

The Whale Coming Close to Shore

60 x 20cm / 24 x 8in

I chose to use unpainted cane in *The Whale Coming Close to Shore* as its natural colour combined well with my palette and the lengths of cane reminded me of the masts of old sailing ships. Reminiscent of sails, I threaded cane between pieces of cloth to hold the fabric in a particular shape, and secured it by sewing along each side of the cane to make a sleeve. The ridge and shadow made by the stitching then became part of the composition.

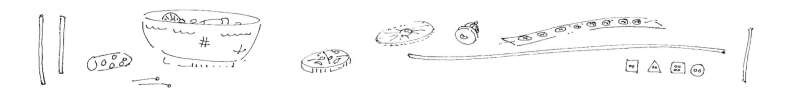

Occasionally an added object is of such interest that it demands a picture to be made for itself. Having found this little bird in a specialist bead shop I felt compelled to give it a home.

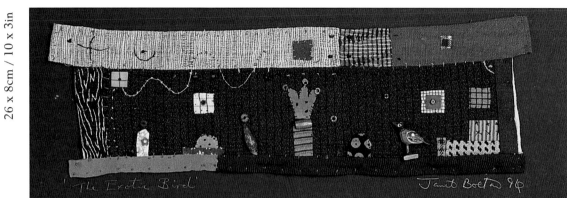

26 x 8cm / 10 x 3in

Exotic Bird

Buttons are a great passion of mine. I am amazed to think how such a tiny item can be a clear and distilled indicator of a specific style and period. Buttons as we know them date back to the fourteenth century and encompass every material and method of construction including wood, glass, enamel, mother of pearl, precious stones, bone, metal and fabric. Their history fascinates me, and I take great pleasure in imagining the circumstance of each. A simple card of buttons bought from a department store can give me as much pleasure as a precious, collectible antique.

I have a considerable collection and some years ago felt that I wanted to make a picture in honour of these undervalued safeguards of human modesty.

I had intended to use cane in *Favourite Buttons and Pieces of Old Fabric* to create a grid to display my favourite buttons and fabrics, but when placed between the objects, the cane looked too heavy. I needed a much lighter solution. I finally replaced it with couched lines of cotton thread. Thread was also in keeping with the original intention of the picture, of using only materials associated with needlework. Sometimes, after trying many alternatives, the solution seems so obvious and simple that you can't imagine why you didn't think of it in the first place.

28 x 28cm / 11 x 11in

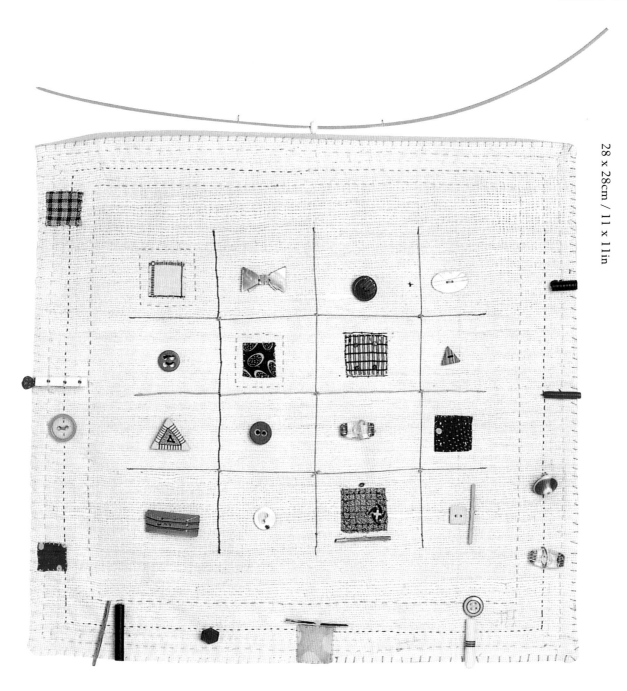

Favourite Buttons and Pieces of Old Fabric

9 5

40.5 x 28cm / 16 x 11in

The Tiger Box

A small collection of painted, wooden figurines from India inspired me to explore the theme of tigers. I echoed the unusual, diagonal stripes of the little wooden carvings in my tiger, and painted the cane lengths in a motley red, black and yellow. Finally, in an effort to make all the elements relate to the theme I completed the picture with a tin of Tiger Balm, a fiery, all-purpose cure from Asia.

Unusual and commonplace objects can find their place in your work. In *Northern Waters*, the bone fish threaded onto the cane are North American Indian artefacts. The two fish swimming are cut from the base of a Camembert cheese box that I painted, and then marked with an indelible pen. The two long beads at the end of the cane are broken pieces of sailors' clay pipes which my children used to hunt for on the banks of the Thames at low tide.

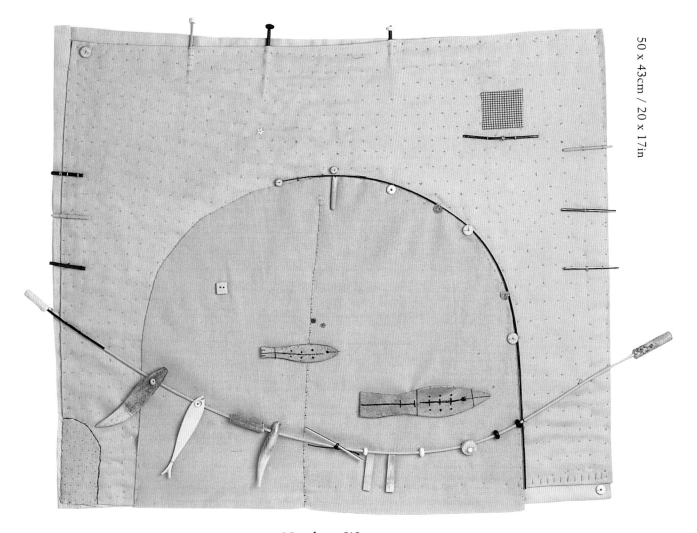

50 x 43cm / 20 x 17in

Northern Waters

20 x 6.5cm / 8 x 2¹/₂in

Special Pieces
Special Pieces *was completed with a porcupine quill.*

A model makers' shop is another good source of interesting bits and pieces that you may find work well with your pictures. There you will find an array of small brass fittings for model sailboats, tiny portholes, minute lengths of knotted rope, miniature aeroplane propellers. Their tiny proportions are just right for the scale of my work.

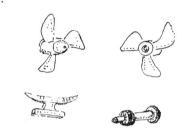

Fittings for model sailboats

These shops also carry a marvellous selection of local and exotic wood cut into delicate strips, and quite perfect for juxtaposing with fabric. Inspired by board games old and new, I used thin strips of balsa wood to create an imaginary game in *Board Games*. A small collection of bone counters fit beautifully into the picture. I had other wooden game counters with numbers carved on them that I was desperate to include, but they were just too big and had to be put aside. Perhaps they will find their place in another picture to be made some time in the future. If an added object is placed in your picture as an essential part of the composition, its original meaning will become secondary to its function in the arrangement of shapes. Its true meaning only emerges on closer inspection, often revealing a hidden joke.

40 x 40cm / 16 x 16in

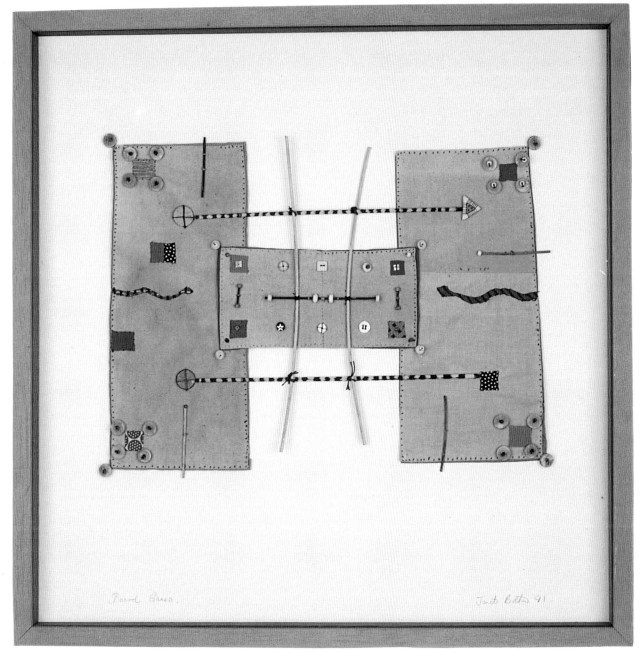

Board Games

I am always on the look-out for interesting objects to include in my pictures but rarely do I buy or collect with a specific picture in mind. Haberdashery stores are a great source of braids, beads, buttons and all the accoutrements of dressmaking. If you have never spent time in a well-stocked haberdashery you will be amazed at the wealth of fascinating paraphernalia that can be incorporated into your pictures. Jumble sales, charity shops, market stands from junk to antique can all provide wonderful hunting grounds. Old, rarely worn necklaces can be plundered and garments looted for their buttons and buckles. There is no need to spend a fortune, and it is so satisfying recycling materials.

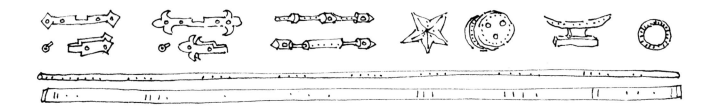

MAKING A SEED BOX

The Workshop Box

1. When I was a child living in the countryside in the North of England, one of the perennial games that swept through the playground along with skipping, hopscotch and my favourite, wooden tops, was collecting seed trays. We arranged and carefully labelled the different seeds on cotton wool in box lids. It's an activity I've continued, one way or another, all my life, and I can't resist collecting bits and pieces and arranging them in patterns. *The Workshop Box* is a direct descendant from my seed box days. This picture was inspired by Sandra Drew of The Drew Gallery in Canterbury. She sent all her artists a cigar box with the same request – to do whatever they liked following the Victorian tradition of painting on cigar box lids. As I wasn't painting, but did use cigar boxes to store my bits and pieces, *The Workshop Box* was my contribution.

Why not make your own 'seed boxes' with all your favourite objects?

2. If you have been working on a picture, it is now time for you to consider the final touches that will complete it. If you haven't already decided on what you want to 'add', try spending a lot of time in front of your picture and let it speak to you. You may find that your picture is complete without any further additions. If this is the case, then let it be.

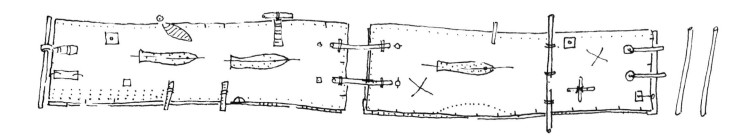

Framing Your Picture

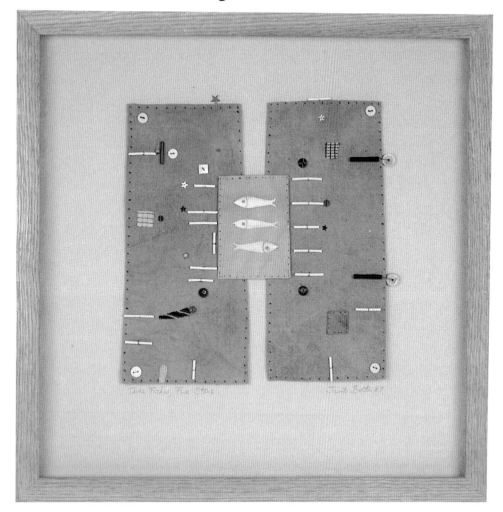

25 x 25cm / 10 x 10in

Three Fishes, Five Stars

For me, framing my work has several vital functions – it protects the work, it defines the work, and most importantly it reasserts my intention of using fabric to make pictures that are intended to hang on a wall.

The way in which a picture is framed is an important extension of the picture-making process. A badly framed picture can lose its impact.

Fabrics pressed under conventional framing will eventually deteriorate, and for this reason you should use a deep box frame with a spacer. The spacer is the device that holds the glass or perspex away from the picture. A box frame provides a practical and aesthetic solution to framing fabric pictures. Fabric needs space to breathe, and in some way the picture itself is an object, so framing it in a box seems right and appropriate.

Use acid-free mount boards in preference to untreated card. Over time, fabric will stain and eventually rot if laid onto poor quality paper. As paper ages, the destructive chemicals used in its manufacture leach out, and will cause untold damage to your pictures. To give myself more choice, I often use manufactured fabric-covered mounting boards. These unfortunately have not been treated, so to protect my picture I place a piece of acid-free paper between the picture and the mounting board. All these materials are readily available at art shops.

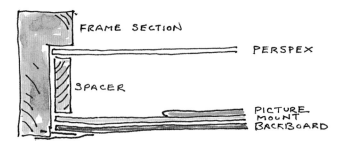

Cross section

As you can see from the illustration the spacer stops the glass from holding the picture in place, so some other way has to be found to secure the mount board. An easy solution is to continue sewing. Place the acid-free paper, then your picture on the mount board, and using a large needle with a narrow head, simply sew them together with tiny stitches at the front and larger stitches at the back.

The Dale Bred Ram

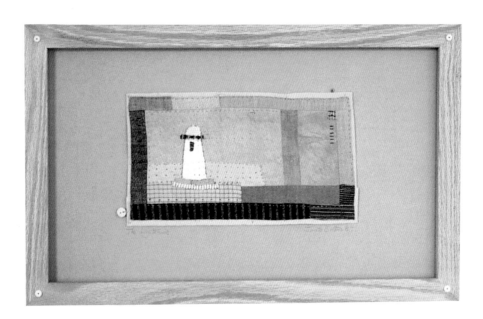

Small Lighthouse

I find it very difficult to visualize how my picture will look when framed, so I place it on many different shapes and sizes of mounting board before making a final decision. There is a general picture framer's rule of thumb: the smaller the picture the larger the mount. The contrast emphasizes the quality of a very small piece. Even when using a professional framer, it is a good idea to have tried some alternatives first.

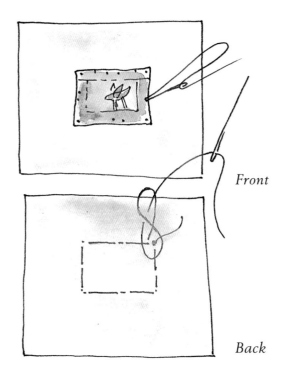

Front

Back

Similarly when choosing your moulding, take your time. Place your picture against a selection of frames and consider the effect each has on it. I prefer plain wooden mouldings, and sometimes paint them to complement a particular picture. There is a great variety of surface textures and paint effects that you can choose from, and you may want to explore several possibilities before you commit yourself.

If you live in a clean environment you could dispense with either glass or perspex. Frame your picture to give it definition but omit the covering; in this way the quality of the cloth remains undiminished.

In most situations, however, a protective covering is unavoidable. Perspex cuts out more damaging ultra-violet rays than glass; it is lighter in weight and does not break, but it does scratch easily.

Once your picture is framed and ready to be hung, keep in mind that fabrics fade quickly, so avoid putting it where sunlight will shine on it. If you have 'quilted' your picture one more consideration must be taken into account – very strong, side lighting can emphasize the furrows made by quilting. The shadows produced can be so strong that the lines will dominate all other aspects of the picture, making it difficult to 'read'.

The Fish Kite

CHAPTER TEN

Step-by-step ~ Four Flowers

15 x 15cm / 6 x 6in

Four Flowers (actual size)

In this chapter I will be presenting step-by-step directions for making one picture. I have chosen the time-honoured theme of a vase of flowers for it allows for infinite personal variations, and since it has been a popular subject in every age and culture you will have no difficulty in finding plenty of inspirational material to set you off on your own voyage.

You may choose to follow my picture closely or you may prefer to incorporate your own ideas. Even if you decide to adopt my palette, remember to look carefully at your fabrics, side by side, rather than trying to match exactly each item in my picture. My hope is that within the security of these simplified step-by-step instructions you will trust your own judgement to create a picture that is distinctly yours.

Step-by-step

1. Select a foundation fabric.
I used two pieces of the same fabric, each measuring 16.5 x 9cm / 6 1/2 x 3 1/2 in, and joined them to alter the direction of the weave. The seam can be either hand or machine sewn.

2. Select as many small pieces of fabric as you can find for the vase, petals and stems. Check their colour and scale against the foundation fabric and each other to see which work best together.

109

3. Cut and place in position the strips of fabric chosen for the border. Remember to cut the top and bottom border strips marginally longer than the side strips.

4. Join by machine or hand any borders made of more than one strip of fabric and press open.

5. Using 0.6cm / ^{1}/4in seam allowance, machine or hand sew the side borders to the foundation. Press open.

6. Add the top and bottom borders to the foundation and press open.

7. Turn the raw edges under 0.6cm / ^{1}/4in. Press lightly and pin in place.

8. Select a backing cloth, approximately 20 x 20cm / 8 x 8in. The colour is important for this picture as it is placed to remain a visible part of the composition.

111

9. Place the foundation on top of the backing cloth. Turn the edges of the backing in under the foundation, and pin into place using the pins that are holding the hem of the foundation. How much you turn in depends on how much of the backing cloth you want to remain visible.

10. Sew the foundation to the backing cloth by hand, using a small hem stitch. Decide whether you want the stitches to remain unseen, or whether you want to create a pattern with the stitching.

11. Cut out the shapes for the flowers, stems, and leaves. So that you can accurately judge how they will look in your composition cut the shapes to the actual size without a turning-under allowance.

12. Cut out the vase from a fabric scrap measuring approximately 10 x10cm / 4 x 4in.

The vase handles can be made in two ways. Either cut them from separate pieces of fabric to achieve a crisp effect; or if you prefer the softer line in my version, cut the handles as part of the vase, and without any hole. A small snip into the fabric is all you need for turning and making the hole in the centre of each handle.

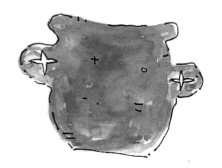

13. Arrange all the shapes until you are pleased with your composition. Don't pin your shapes down – the fabric pieces will adhere to each other and it leaves you free to move your shapes with ease.

14. When you are happy with your composition replace the shapes with pieces cut to the same shape, but with a 0.6 cm / $^{1}/4$ inch turning-under allowance all around, and pin into position.

15. Appliqué the vase in place. Where shapes overlap you do not need to secure the base shapes. However, remember to turn the edges of the stems under where the lip of the vase crosses them. You can adjust the shape of the vase as you sew by turning under varying amounts of fabric.

16. Appliqué the stems in position, again remembering to turn under any leaf edges concealed by the stems. As more and more shapes are finalized and refined you may find that you want to adjust and reposition your remaining shapes.

17. Appliqué the petals and then the flower centres in position.

18. Experiment with 'added objects' or other fabric shapes you may care to include, such as the small squares and circles on my picture. Cut out the shapes to finished size and when you are happy with the arrangement replace them with shapes cut larger to allow for turning under. Pin and sew into place.

CHAPTER ELEVEN

Gallery

15 x 10cm / 6 x 4in

One Cow

Having completed one picture you are ready to set off on your own personal journey, exploring those subjects and motifs that are meaningful to you. I am sure that you will gain as much enjoyment and satisfaction from your work as I do from mine.

21.5 x 15.5cm / 8¹/₂ x 6in

The Mill at the Edge of the Moors

12.5 x 10cm / 5 x 4in

Three Flowers

25 x 20cm / 10 x 8in

High Above the Hive

30.5 x 30.5cm / 12 x 12in

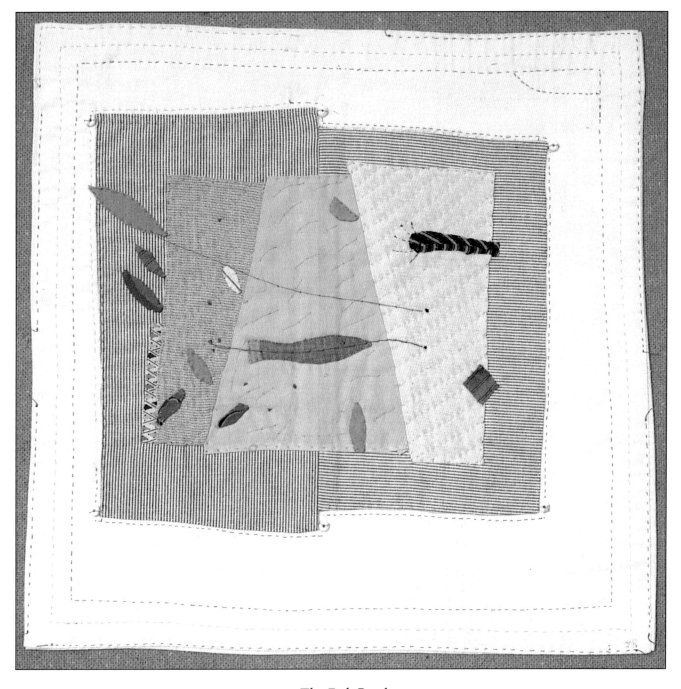

The Fish Pond

CHAPTER TWELVE

Templates

123

Acknowledgements

With many thanks to my editor Ljiljana Ortolja-Baird for her invaluable support and assistance, and to Sandra Lousada for her sensitive photography of my work.

PHOTOGRAPHIC CREDITS

The Fish Kite – Paul Seheult

The Bird and the Tiger – Joël Degen

Three Fishes, Five Stars – Joël Degen

Index

Index